to live with the

fairy folk

to live with the

fairy
folk

a guide to attract benevolent spirits

marina t. stern

WEISER BOOKS
Boston, MA/York Beach, ME

First published in 2002 by
Red Wheel/Weiser, LLC
York Beach, ME
With offices at:
368 Congress Street
Boston, MA 02210
www.redwheelweiser.com

Library of Congress Cataloging-in-Publication Data
Stern, Marina T.
  To live with the fairy folk : a guide to attract benevolent spirits / Marina T. Stern.
    p. cm.
Includes bibliographical references.
  ISBN 1-57863-273-0 (pbk.)
  1. Fairies. 2. Spirits. I. Title.
  BF1552 .S73 2002
  133.1'4--DC21

                                                              2002007181

Illustrations by Patricia Frevert
Typeset in Adobe Garamond
Printed in Canada
TCP

09 08 07 06 05 04 03 02
 8 7 6 5 4 3 2 1

for Tom

thanks for everything.

I know a bank where the wild thyme blows,
Where oxlips and the nodding violet grows,
Quite over-canopied with luscious woodbine,
With sweet musk-roses and with eglantine;
There sleeps Titania sometime of the night,
Lull'd in these flowers with dances and delight;
And there the snake throws her enamell'd skin,
Weed wide enough to wrap a fairy in.

—William Shakespeare,
   A Midsummer Night's Dream

contents

part one:

etiquette and the folk

part two:

habitat for the folk

part three:

magical combinations: sample garden designs

acknowledgments

No book of nonfiction can be written without assistance. While an author slaves over his hot computer in solitude, there are inspirations and support along the way.

A thousand thanks are due to Carodoc ap Cador, who instructed me for two years in the fairy ways. A thousand more to Ed Fitch, who instructed me for nine more years, and gave me my ordination.

To Dan Brogan, who tolerated my hero worship until his death, and nurtured my latent mania for gardening, loving gratitude always.

To Duane Smith, who helped out with a shovel, a saw, or a camera as needed. I never could have done it without him.

Thanks to my editor, Robyn Heisey. Without her enthusiastic support, this volume would have remained no more than a sheaf of notes in a paper folder.

Above all, I need to thank my husband, Tom Stern. For teaching me to use a computer, for doing all the computing that was beyond my skill, for giving me time and space to work, and for just plain believing in me.... What can I say? Meet you under the walnut tree.

introduction

Who are the Fair Folk and why would I want to live with them?

THERE ARE AS MANY theories about the origins and identity of the Folk as there are people who believe in their existence. There are even more, as each folklorist has her pet theories, whether or not she believes in the objects of her study. Further, it is possible to hold many competing beliefs simultaneously, as they are not mutually exclusive.

Here I list some of the more common beliefs:

The Folk are the previous human inhabitants of the land, reduced by the retelling of their stories with cumulative inaccuracies over many generations.

The Folk are the gods of indigenous religions, still remembered, but no longer given the status of gods.

The Folk are the spirits of a place, Nature made manifest.

The Folk are projections of human wishes, human psyche.

The Folk are the characters from stories told to children, to warn them away from danger.

The Folk are prescientific attempts to understand natural phenomena.

The Folk are the souls of the dead.

The Folk are a race midway between the spiritual and the material.

The Folk are fallen angels.

Which of these theories, if any, are true? I suspect that they all are. The Folk are made of memory, imagination, tradition, and desire. They exist wherever people exist and wherever they used to exist. They travel with people and stay where they have been. For instance, in the Danish-American town of Solvang, California, many types of Folk may be found. There are the remnants of the companions of the original Native American tribes. The Spanish missionaries left their traces as well, in the missions that bookend the town. The Danish Folk are not only locally celebrated, but also visible, peering from shop window and sidewalk garden alike. If I were to move there, the companions of my ancestors would go with me, Irish and Spanish and African and Caribbean. We leave nothing behind.

Why would you want to live with the Folk? That may not be the relevant question. The Folk are ever present, like air. What I propose to accomplish, with this book, is to give an outline of the kinds of behavior and surroundings that will cause the Folk to regard you favorably. To be surrounded by cheerful Folk is to be cheerful oneself, buoyed up by the laughter of Nature Herself. To arrange your life, home, and especially garden, in order to make the Folk welcome, is to welcome happiness, luck, and love.

There are unfriendly Folk as well, with whom you would not wish to consort. For example, the Scottish water horse devours those who attempt to ride it. The bogart is less malevolent. He makes a nuisance of himself by spilling milk and throwing things at children, in the manner of a poltergeist.

The best defense against them is to surround yourself with friendly Folk, and treat them well. The Folk are scrupulously just, by their own measure of justice, and will not countenance the mistreatment of their favorites.

Why do I use the term "the Folk," instead of simply saying "fairies"? Political correctness. Some of the Folk, in some cultures, find the term "fairies" offensive. In both Scandinavia and Scotland, the word "fairy" was a fighting word. To refer to the Folk in any but the most respectful terms was to invite shipwreck, epidemics among the livestock, and the kidnapping of children. Rule Number One in making friends with anyone is to avoid insulting him. I do, however, use the term "fairy" as an adjective when indicating something traditionally associated with the Folk, as in the phrase, "fairy tree."

Other common and acceptable ways of referring to the Folk include "the Good People," "the Little People," "the Good Neighbors," "the Gentry," and "the People of Peace."

part one

etiquette and the folk

respect for fairy privacy

THE MOST IMPORTANT FACTOR in attracting the Fair Folk to your surroundings is yourself. Your behavior and attitudes will have a greater impact on the attractiveness of your home and garden than any plant or ornament you can place there.

If you wish the Fair Folk to be at home in your garden, you must respect their privacy. Just as you would not like to have your human neighbors peeking over the fence and into your windows, the Folk do not want you to spy on them. You must resist the temptation to locate the source of quiet rustling under the hedges or giggling behind the shrubs.

Go about your work quietly in the garden. Spend leisure time there as well. Bring a book or your needlework into the garden and proceed to read or stitch. The Folk will, in time, become accustomed to your presence, and gradually begin to show themselves.

Allow spaces for naturalness in the garden. If you put in lights, for example, keep them to the paths and buildings. Allow the beds and borders to be lit only by the moon and the stars, lest you keep the Folk away. You need not be too strict about keeping the edges of your lawn well trimmed. The lower branches of your shrubs need not be too well pruned. The Folk thrive on a modicum of disorder outdoors.

generosity

THE FOLK ARE FOND of people who are openhanded and open-hearted.

Do not put netting over your fruit trees, if you wish to attract the Folk. Instead, plant enough to share with the birds, and with the Folk, who are their companions.

Let the Folk see your dealings with others, and keep those dealings warm. Throw parties outdoors when the weather is good, and be sure that there is plenty to eat and drink. Linger outside when your party is over; you will feel the presence of the Folk. You might hear them, as well, but do not eavesdrop. Enjoy the awareness of their presence that they give you, but ask for no more.

Find, or place, a flat stone in the most secret part of your yard, and leave gifts for the Folk there. They favor the first ripe fruit from each tree, a bit of milk, a piece of fresh bread. Do not insult the Folk by leaving food that is stale or imperfect. If you see birds or squirrels taking what you have left, know that this is the form in which the Folk have chosen to accept your gifts. Place fresh food out each day. It need not be fancy. Bread is valued as much as croissants, if it is fresh, and kindly intended. Make sure there is always fresh water available, as well.

Never, however, leave gifts of clothing for the Folk, unless it is your intention to be rid of them. Gifts of clothing cause some of the most helpful Folk, the ones who assist with the housework and scare away burglars, to leave, never to return. It is the equivalent of buying them out of a contract. Others are offended by the idea that their human hosts disapprove of their nakedness. In either case, we lose their company.

Put up bird feeders, and keep them full. Put up birdhouses as well, and clean them seasonally. Let your whole garden show the influence of your giving heart.

The Folk have been known to reward generosity, well . . . generously. A modest gift, freely given and witnessed by the Folk, has been rewarded with inexhaustible wealth. Instances of this kind have been recorded in widely separated cultures. For instance, there is a Japanese tale of an elderly woodcutter who was kind to an injured sparrow. The sparrow threw him an extravagant party for his kindness, and gave him a box of gold and precious gems. The woodcutter's greedy wife then found the same sparrow, and demanded a present. The sparrow gave her a box of demons.

In a Scottish tale, a wealthy man promised a mug of ale to a child of the Folk. The boy drained the entire contents of the gentleman's cellar into his mug. The gentleman did not complain of having been tricked, but bore his loss graciously. Years later, when the gentleman was being held as a prisoner of war, the boy released him.

Another Scottish tale tells of a miser who sought to increase his wealth by stealing fairy treasure. The Folk rewarded him with a life-long case of arthritis.

kindness

THE FOLK VALUE KINDNESS in the people with whom they share space. Be gentle and loving with your spouse, your children, your pets. The Folk do not understand or appreciate "tough love." Quarreling is as inimical to the Folk as rudeness or greed.

Rescuing a pet from the pound, or a baby bird that has been pushed from the nest, is behavior much esteemed by the Folk.

Keeping pest control within the realm of kindness can be a problem. Anything done to kill snails will not be appreciated by the snails, whether or not it is organic, nontoxic, or otherwise politically correct. I step on them and accept the karma. I love my plants more than I love the snails.

My folkloric sources are silent on the subject of pest control. Surely, farmers in every age have used whatever means were effective and available to protect their crops. There are no European legends in which the Folk have punished farmers for killing snails, grasshoppers, aphids, and the like.

On the other hand, there are many tales of people who have been punished for cruelty to mammals and birds. For this reason,

I recommend non-lethal methods for controlling rabbits, gophers, and similar pests.

Whenever possible, control pests by discouraging them, rather than by committing pesticide. Use scarecrows, flash tape, tall fences. Almost any dog will serve to scare away rabbits, even if he is no hunter.

For example, gophers are a big problem in my part of the country. There is documented evidence that the Russian colonists in Northern California during the nineteenth century blamed the gophers for the failure of their colony. Of course, their complete lack of farming skills and the unpleasantness regarding enslaving the indigenous residents may have been contributing factors, but they did not want to admit to that. Better to blame the gophers.

The most common means of gopher control include poison gas, poison bait, and lethal traps. Use of these means will, of course, convince the Folk that you are a bloodthirsty and evil soul who should be either avoided or punished.

This is not the impression you want to give the Folk, nor do you want to expose your children or pets to the risks involved. If peaceful coexistence is not an option (gophers will eat every trace of root off a rosebush or young fruit tree, leaving it to lie flat on the ground, dying), plant your tasty-rooted plants in solid containers aboveground. Gophers will chew right through flimsy containers. As an alternative, plant them in the ground in a wire basket. Spraying the entire yard with a commercially available castor oil emulsion may bring their presence down to a tolerable level, but can be expensive, and must be repeated every few months.

Many authorities write that gophers can be kept out of a garden by surrounding it with poisonous or unsavory plants, such as euphorbia, daffodils, or sage. I have tried this method. It does not work, not even a little. Gophers can cheerfully burrow five, ten, even fifteen feet deep in order to avoid these barriers. The same holds true for mechanical barriers, such as buried fencing. Save the effort.

Note that roses and many other shrubs that have been damaged by gophers can be rerooted successfully by pruning them severely and burying the stump of the root in potting soil. Keep it moist and shaded until it is well established, a matter of a few months.

What do I do? I spray with castor oil, reroot the casualties in pots, and keep a dachshund.

chapter four
neatness

As a confirmed slob, I consider the emphasis the Folk place on neatness completely irrational. Nevertheless, there it is: all the traditional folkloric sources agree that the Folk value a tidy home, a well swept hearth. Since the physical manifestation of spiritual energies is nonrational on its face, the Folk are certainly welcome to demonstrate whatever preferences they choose.

The Folk prefer that the floors be swept and mopped, the dishes washed and put away, before the family retires for the night. The Folk consider sloppiness a major moral fault. They are reputed to pinch "casual" housekeepers, such as myself, to the point of bruising. They are also reputed to reward neat housekeepers with lasting prosperity and happiness.

Folk tradition does not address the feelings of the Folk toward vacuum cleaners, but I am sure that they despise leaf blowers.

Keep the weeds pulled and the lawns edged, in order to welcome the Folk. Of course, one man's weed is another man's wildflower, so you need not carry weeding to a fanatical extreme. Personally, I consider that the local birds and squirrels have as much say in the landscape as I have. Rather than automatically removing bird-planted material, I consider its appropriateness for the site. It was the birds' idea, not mine, that my first garden should include hollyhocks. They worked out nicely.

chapter five

fairness

THE FOLK HAVE A KEEN sense of justice. It is vital that one hoping to gain their favor keep his promises and honor his contracts.

The Folk are omnipresent, even in urban areas, even when they are not detectable by our senses. One must keep this in mind when doing business. Attempting to gain unfair advantage, inflicting hardship on another, and acting with dishonesty disgust the Folk.

They reward tradesmen who perform good work at a fair price. The Folk dispense luck, so it is within their jurisdiction to do so. Dishonest dealing is handled in a most Draconian manner, not excluding death by "accident."

Do not be carried away by nursery visions of the Folk. The Folk are both light and dark, and manifest all the aspects of Nature's psyche. Much of the traditional lore addressing the Folk is concerned with avoiding their displeasure, or avoiding them altogether.

chapter six

romance

THE FOLK LOOK ON ROMANCE with great favor. As they are, in one aspect, the remnants of fertility gods, they are heartily in favor of warm relations between the sexes.

Ironically, as puritanical as the Folk are about neatness in housekeeping and fair dealing in business, they are indifferent to issues of monogamy and fidelity. They do not care much who is kissing whom, as long as there is plenty of kissing going on.

The males of the Folk have long been accused of seducing lonely mortal women. The females of the Folk rarely actively attempt the seduction of human men, but human men have often succeeded in trapping women of the Folk into marriage. *These relationships always end badly.* Platonic friendships and mutually beneficial business relationships* between mortals and the Folk can be rewarding on many levels, but romances with the Folk always end in heartache. Frequently, they spell the end of all joy for the inevitably jilted mortal.

That warning given, place a comfortable bench in a private corner of the garden. Frequent it with a romantic associate of your own, and you will be rewarded with the sound of silvery laughter all around.

---

* I know a story about a man who traded whiskey with a merman, but that is not relevant here.

love-talker

Lonesome young women who do not have sweethearts tend to spend much of their time mooning about outdoors. When they do so, they may attract the attentions of the Love-Talker. He is a handsome and charming sprite, who swiftly induces the woman to fall irrevocably in love with him. The Love-Talker abandons her within a few weeks or months, since it is the process that he values, and not the woman. The woman then pines away, unable to accept the loss of her immortal sweetheart, or to find a man who can measure up to his romantic ways.

Sea people

At least two species of sea folk—the Selkies and the Mermaids—are known to interact romantically with mortals.

The Selkies, also known as the Roan, are Folk in the shape of human beings. In the water, they are able to assume the form of seals. Their native territory is a dry land under the sea, where they live and work in the same manner in which mortals live in their lands.

The old ballad "The Great Silkie of Sule Skerrie" tells the story of a male Selkie who rapes a woman and leaves her pregnant. Years later, he returns to claim his son. Both father and son are then killed by the husband of the abused and abandoned woman. It is not a happy tale, but it is a lovely song.

The more usual tale is that a man steals the sealskin of a woman of the Selkies while she is on mortal shores. Without her sealskin, she is unable to return to her own country, and so is compelled to marry her captor. As she is pretty, affectionate, and sweet-natured, her husband is happy with her. He forgets that she is a captive, rather than a willing partner. Eventually, she finds her sealskin and returns to her own country, without a word of farewell.

The Mermaids, while well-intentioned, are more dangerous. When a mermaid falls in love with a mortal man, it is more usual for her to pull him into the sea, thus drowning him, than to join him on land.

On the other hand, a platonic relationship with the sea people can be largely beneficial. More than one family of hereditary healers was founded by the blessing of a friendly mermaid or merman. The Old Man of Cury, as he was known, rescued a mermaid who had been stranded on shore by the falling tide. She taught him to cure illnesses and reverse curses. The skill remained in his family for several generations.

In a similar story, after promising Lutey the gift of healing, the mermaid he had rescued tried to drown him. He escaped by means of magic. His descendants did receive the ability to cure illnesses, but once every nine years, one of their number died at sea.

fairy royalty

Very rarely, a queen or princess of the Folk takes a fancy to a mortal man and selects him to be her consort. In these instances, the man goes to his Lady's court to attend her. Generally, he might as well forget about resuming his old life, should things sour between him and his fair mistress. A time anomaly separates Faerie and the mortal realm. One who visits Faerie and returns finds he has been gone for approximately three hundred times longer than he supposed. A person returning from an overnight visit to Faerie finds that a year has passed. A besotted lover who stays in Faerie for a year and returns to the mortal realm finds himself a dimly remembered legend. With no connections to the current world, these travelers quickly die of loneliness and old age.

part two

habitat for the folk

chapter seven
fairy trees

THE FOLK ARE KNOWN to make their own food by means of glamour, out of mushrooms and leaves. Nonetheless, the person who wishes to curry favor with the Folk should make abundant food available to them.

Aside from the flat stone mentioned earlier, on which you lay daily gifts of milk, water, and baked goods, it is good to have plenty of flowering trees and shrubs. In a frost-free climate, I aim to have ripe fruit available in the garden twelve months out of the year. This is not as difficult as it sounds. Many citrus fruits, and other subtropicals, ripen in the winter. Of course, you must work with the climate nature has given you, and work within its limitations. Combine, as well you can, early and late varieties of fruits suitable to your environment. The folk will notice your effort, and approve.

In a garden designed to be attractive to the Folk, all plants are best grown organically. Rather than relying on toxins to control diseases and pests, use tonics drawn from the folk tradition. I have included a list of sources for recipes for such tonics in the Recommended Reading section. In addition to being free of toxins, and therefore safe to use around children, pets, and the Folk, they usually have the advantage of being inexpensive to use and just as effective as their poisonous alternatives.

Many trees are listed in the traditional sources as being attractive to the Folk. Most of them are also attractive to birds and other wildlife as well. Some of them are food trees that have long contributed to the survival of human communities.

The triad of oak, ash, and thorn is known from songs and tales carried down over centuries. If these three trees grow together, on the top of a hill away from any others, that place is certain to be a major center of supernatural influence.

Oak: Genus *Quercus*

All species and varieties are attractive to the Folk. Pick one according to your tastes and its suitability to your soil and climate. I am most fond of the deciduous oaks with deeply lobed leaves that turn bright colors in autumn, but that is just me.

If you are lucky enough to have a mature native oak on your property, cherish it. It is already home to the Folk, and has been since before you were born. An oak that has stood for centuries can be killed in short order with improper care, so ask an experienced local gardener how to care for yours. Most agricultural universities have phone-in lines manned by expert gardeners. Look in the gardening section of your local newspaper to find out the number. Where I live, the secrets to maintaining a native oak tree are these:

> Do not change the level of the soil between the trunk and the dripline.

Do not water or feed the tree between the dripline and the trunk.

Do not even *think* about planting anything under the oak.

Oaks planted by the gardener are easier to maintain, and grow quickly. They take a long time to develop true character, though. Do not expect too much too soon.

*A*sh: Genus *Fraxinus*

This is the tree known in the United States as the ash. It is not to be confused with the mountain ash, which will be treated separately.

Different species of *Fraxinus* grow throughout the country. All the ones with which I am familiar are tall and graceful. They make good shade trees, if there are no overhead wires to interfere. Planting an ash tree with the intention of pruning it later to avoid overhead lines is pointless, as an ash tree that has been topped loses all its native grace.

Some varieties seed themselves profusely. If you plant one of these, you and all your neighbors will spend many summer hours in the backbreaking labor of digging out seedling trees. Use a sterile variety, if you can find one. This will not make the tree less attractive to the Folk. Unlike other trees, the ash is not attractive because of its seeds.

Hawthorn: Genus *Cratægus*

This is the tree that is called simply "thorn" in old poems and tales. This may be to simplify rhyme and meter, or perhaps the language has changed. Indeed, greater acquaintance with the wider world forces language to change. In my native California, as in Africa, a thorn tree that is not identified further is presumed to be an acacia.

Hawthorn is a pretty tree with flowers in the spring and berries in the summer and fall. It is a member of the rose family, and, like all roses, is well loved by the Folk. I have read nostalgic accounts of gathering the fruit, called "haws," in order to make juice or jelly. The fruit is also attractive to birds, for whom it is a valuable winter food source.

It is native to the eastern parts of this country, as well as to Europe, and so is well adapted to the climate of the Northeast. The good news is that it can tolerate cold winters. The bad news is that it does not thrive in frost-free climates. Most varieties are susceptible to fireblight, a devastating bacterial disease. If fireblight is a problem in your area, it would be wise to look for resistant cultivars, as there is no cure. I have found folk remedies to be ineffective.

Rowan: Genus *Sorbus*

The lovely rowan tree, beloved by the Folk, is the same as that known in this country as the mountain ash. It is grown for its clusters of white flowers, lacy foliage, and brightly colored fruit. In some species, the fruit hangs on through the winter, making it a good source of food for winter birds. It is a tough tree, tolerant of wind, drought, cold, and heat. Like the hawthorn, it requires a chilly winter and is susceptible to fireblight. That it should share this weakness should come as no surprise. After all, it is also a member of the rose family.

This is only one of many red-berried trees loved by the Folk. There are fewer stories of uncanny kidnappings associated with the rowan than with most other fairy trees. It may, for this reason, be a safer choice for gardens frequented by children or adults of poor judgment.

Apple: Genus *Malus*

Apple trees represent power and youth. They are attractive to the Folk throughout the year, and in all stages of growth. By choosing the rootstock on which your tree is grafted, you control the ultimate size of the tree. Apple trees are available ranging from four-foot-tall bushes suitable for growing in a pot on an apartment balcony, to giant trees suitable for climbing. Depending on variety, they can thrive and produce everywhere from Maine to Los Angeles. This is no exaggeration. Four of the five varieties of apples I planted two years ago are already bearing, and I garden in one of the hotter suburbs of Los Angeles. The earliest begins to bloom in January, the latest in May, yielding five months of glorious blooms in delicate pinks and whites.

Some apples are self-fertile. Others require the presence of a "friend" of another variety in order to produce. Local nurseries will be able to tell you which is which, as will any good mail-order catalog. Note an important clue: if a source cannot or will not tell you whether a variety is self-fertile, it is not a good one.

Like the rowan and the hawthorn, the apple is a member of the rose family. Most of its susceptibility to fireblight has been bred out, and is not a serious problem. If it becomes a problem in your garden, remove the tree and start over with a different cultivar.

Those who fall asleep under an apple tree are subject to kidnapping by the Folk for amorous purposes. If you would like to try the experiment, have a four-leafed clover in your pocket for protection. Do not eat or drink anything offered to you by the Folk . . . unless you prefer not to return.

Hazel: Genus *Corylus*

Hazel represents wisdom and fertility. The Salmon of Knowledge known from European folklore gained its power by eating the hazelnuts that had fallen into its pool.

Hazelnuts are a major cash crop, here in the West, under their alias of filberts. They grow well in most of the United States, but a fungal disease limits their range in the East. Check with a local university to find out whether it will be a problem in your area.

In addition to being attractive to the Folk and conducive to wisdom and fertility, hazelnuts are also delicious with chocolate.

Holly: Genus *Ilex*

Holly is also well loved for its red berries, as well as for its glossy, evergreen leaves. It is the plant specially dedicated to the midwinter holidays, and to their patron, Santa Claus. Any sign that the "right jolly old elf" is welcome is a good thing, as I am sure you will agree.

Although the berries are not tasty, holly is an important food plant for winter birds. Indeed, if you provide food for wild birds, it is as important to include berries that are not yummy as those that are. Birds, like most of us, eat the things they like best first. If only delicious food is available in your yard, there will be nothing left to attract and sustain them later in the winter.

There are varieties of holly suitable for almost any climate, and in almost any size. They are not susceptible to disease. Any insect problems they develop can be controlled organically. In order to have berries, you must plant both male and female plants. Ask the nurseryman for assistance if you have any questions. I have found that the male and female plants are usually clearly labeled.

Willow: Genus *Salix*

Willow is attractive to the wilder sort of Folk, not the familiar brownies or Blessed Host. It has a slightly sinister reputation and is avoided at night by those who believe in uncanny events, but I have not heard any contemporary accounts of problems associated with its presence. The solitary Folk who inhabit willows can be friendly or unfriendly. A person walking by may not be able to tell whether it is safe to trust a given sprite.

Because of the abundance of growth hormones in its tissues, willow not only roots easily from cuttings, it causes other plants to root more easily as well. If you wish to experiment, put cuttings of the plants you wish to propagate in a glass of water with some cuttings of willow. Pot them up when roots appear.

There are willows to suit any yard, from dwarfs to large shade trees. Most require abundant water, but there are some that will thrive in the desert. Disease is rarely a problem, but most are prone to bugs. It is a major chore to spray a large tree for an insect infestation, so you may want to choose a smaller one, if you do not have access to a cherry picker to assist with the spraying.

The best thing about willows is that, no matter how large your yard is, you only have to buy one. Plant the one in your yard the first season and let it grow. When it is dormant in winter, prune it. Arrange the branches in a vase of water in your living room. By the time you tire of the arrangement, the branches will have rooted. Pot them up. In a few months, they will be ready to plant in the yard: dozens of plants for the price of one, with very little work and almost no skill involved.

The best-known medicinal use of willow is as a source of salicylic acid, a proto-aspirin compound used by indigenous peoples for pain and fever. Any plant with active medicinal properties would naturally have magical associations and magic implies the involvement of the Folk.

Elder: Genus *Sambucus*

The elder is more commonly referred to as the elderberry in the United States. This may seem perfectly self-explanatory, but until I did the research for this book, I thought I had never seen an elder.

After much reading and combing of sources, I realized that the magical elder of song and story is the same large shrub or small tree that I have admired in wild places all my life. There is one growing in the back corner of my yard. It grows natively here, so I like to imagine that my specimen predates the neighborhood.

The elder, in spring, covers itself with large clusters of tiny white flowers, which are visible on moonlit evenings from hundreds of yards away. It is one of our showiest natives, and would be worth growing even if its only virtue were the beauty of its flowers. In addition, its flowers are followed by clusters of berries of red, blue, or purple-black, which are nearly as attractive. It provides food for wildlife. If left unpruned, the tangled branches of the elder shrub also provide first-rate shelter for those same birds and animals. It can be pruned into a tree, and its hollow shoots made into whistles with which to call the Folk.

Elders are rarely available in nurseries, possibly because they are so common and easy to grow. If you see one in a neighbor's yard, ask whether you may dig up a seedling. This is not an imposition. You will be helping with her weeding.

The berries of some species are reputed to be good for pies and winemaking, but I recommend caution. My reference lists the berries of at least one species as "probably poisonous." I prefer to leave the berries to the birds, and enjoy the elder for its visual beauty alone. However, if you are growing a species that you know produces edible berries, the blossoms are edible as well. Dip them into a tempura batter and fry them until crispy and golden. The berries make an old-fashioned wine, suitable for nostalgic musings.

The tree is especially esteemed as a shelter for *friendly* Folk. This is in contrast to other trees, such as oak and willow, which bear about them an aura of awe rather than comfort.

Generalities regarding fairy trees

Nut trees in general are powerful fertility symbols, which makes them favorites of the Folk. A couple hoping for children could do worse than to rendezvous under a walnut tree.

Most nut trees need to be planted in groups of at least two varieties or seedlings, in order to bear a crop. A barren nut tree has no good magic to it. It is the nuts that attract the Folk, just as they attract squirrels and birds.

All stone fruit trees, such as apricots, peaches, cherries, plums, and their hybrids, are attractive to the Folk throughout the year. In the spring there are flowers, in the summer, shade and fruit. In autumn and winter, the tree continues to provide shelter and structure.

It is highly desirable to have fruit ripening throughout the growing season. For this reason, in addition to the usual apples and stone fruits, and the ubiquitous (in California) citrus, I grow loquats, which ripen here in winter or earliest spring, and persimmons, which ripen late in the autumn and hang on the tree into winter. The persimmon tree, in particular, is popular with the Folk, in their guise of hummingbirds. A rich and varied ecosystem can nurture and absorb exotic immigrants, whether they be parrots or pixies.

General rules for the care of fairy trees

Any tree that is patronized by the Folk must be treated with respect.

Water trees appropriately, according to their type:

- Water local natives rarely, if ever.

- Water non-natives according to the advice of local gardeners, or books written by people gardening in a similar climate to yours.

Feed trees appropriately, according to type:

- Give local natives an occasional shovel of compost or composted manure.

- Give non-native shade trees a balanced fertilizer once per year, as directed on the package.

- Give fruit trees a balanced fertilizer three to four times per year, as directed on the package.

Prune trees as necessary:

- Prune out deadwood as you notice it, at least once per year. This is equivalent to a haircut or manicure. It improves the tree's appearance without hurting it at all.

- When you need to cut live wood, which is moist with a green underbark, explain to the tree why you are doing it, and apologize. The traditional formula is, "Old Lady, give me your wood, and I will give you mine, when I become a tree."

- Do your pruning between sunrise and sunset. As comfortable as early dawn and late dusk are for working, they are also favored times for the Folk to engage in feasting, dancing, and romancing their favorites. They will resent your intrusion if you blunder about with loppers and saws while they are arranging their amours. Dawn and dusk are better spent enjoying the flowers, perhaps sharing a pastry and a beverage with the Folk. Be sure you are the one to provide the refreshments. Partaking of fairy food is never without risk.

fairy manifestations and companions

YOU MAY HAVE NOTICED that I frequently note, when describing a tree traditionally associated with the Folk, whether a tree is useful to the birds. This is neither random nor tangential. A yard that is welcoming to wildlife will be welcoming to the Folk for the very reason that the Folk travel with wildlife. In many cases, they are identical to wildlife.

The Folk are, among other things, the embodied soul of Nature. They draw their life and power from all living things, from birds and squirrels and rose bushes. You are more likely to see one of the Folk in the form of an animal than in any guise that would lead you to say unconditionally, "I saw a fairy today." The Folk can take the form of any being you can imagine, as well as many you cannot. I will focus primarily on the most incontrovertible forms the Folk assume, those of hummingbirds and butterflies.

We are fortunate, in the Americas, to have hummingbirds as barometers of the health and attractiveness of our backyard habitats. Even more sensitive, and worldwide in scope, are butterflies.

The needs of hummingbirds and butterflies are similar, but not identical, to the needs of the Folk. Encouraging the former by meeting their physical needs will greatly increase your chances of attracting the latter. The Folk love pretty flying things as much as we do.

*h*ummingbirds

The ancient Celts said nothing about hummingbirds for the same excellent reason that the Greeks, Egyptians, and Vikings were also silent on the subject. Hummingbirds are entirely absent from the Old World. They are uniquely American, and uniquely magical. The first European explorers who described hummingbirds to their sedentary compatriots were met with derision. It was physically impossible, they were told, for a bird to hover, or fly backward.

The people who were here before the Europeans knew better. They honored the hummingbird for its beauty, agility, speed, and courage. Indeed, more than one American culture identified hummingbirds as the souls of warriors who had died in battle. The Aztec god of war was a fire-breathing hummingbird, an image I find hard to picture. In creation stories of the New World, the hummingbird is the one sent out to see whether the waters had subsided after the universal flood, as the dove went out in the creation stories of the Old World. In the lore of many Native American peoples, the hummingbird plays the role of a swift messenger, a bringer of love and healing.

The English names of several genera of hummingbirds frankly

refer to their magical identity. Two genera are called "woodnymphs." One is called "sylphs," another "sunangels." One comes right out and says it: "fairy." The scientist-explorers who named them were on to something.

Of all magical creatures, hummingbirds are the easiest to attract and observe. Faith, intuition, and second sight are not necessary. Anyone with adequate eyesight can see and enjoy them.

To attract hummingbirds, provide them with water, abundant flowers, suitable shelter, and varied patterns of light and shade.

Water features made to attract hummingbirds should be shallow. Hummingbirds can even bathe in the dew that has collected on a leaf. They especially love to bathe on the fly, zipping through the spray of a fountain or sprinkler at full speed. The sight is unforgettable, well worth the effort of placing a fountain in a sunny spot. If a fountain is not practicable on your site, keep your eyes open when you water your garden, whether by sprinkler, or by hand. Such is the fearlessness of the hummingbird that it will even bathe in the spray of a hand-held hose.

The flowers that hummingbirds love most are tubular in shape, rich in nectar, and red. The redness is optional. In order to make the hummingbirds at home in your yard most quickly, include several flowers that are native to your region. They will be most familiar with these, and actively seeking them. Once they have become accustomed to coming to your yard for the penstemons, fuschias, or whatever else the local hummingbirds like, they will stay for the buddleias, honeysuckles, and lilies you have planted for them.

Hummingbirds like to keep plenty of wing room around them. They are unlikely to enter a thicket to feed. The best way to keep them happy and comfortable is to plant nectar plants at different levels, with plenty of open space around tall specimens. They like to rest in the shady shelter of evergreen trees, then swoop into the sunny zones to feed. The more flowers that you provide, the more time the hummingbirds will spend in your yard. They will provide their own magic, and attract other magical beings.

For the comfort of the hummingbirds, and to make your garden comfortable for the Folk and human visitors as well, provide a balance of sunshine and shade. Flowers bloom most abundantly in full sun. Shade provides more comfortable conditions for relaxation. Balance them according to your individual climate. In a cool region, or one in which persistent cloud cover tempers the effects of full sun, two-thirds sun, or even three-fourths, would be ideal. In a scorching Mediterranean or desert climate, half sun to half shade would be better.

Specific flowers that serve to attract hummingbirds include honeysuckle, aloes, salvias of all sorts, butterfly bush, bottlebrush, and citrus of all kinds. The last two also serve as good places for them to build their nests, if your yard is within their nesting range. There is no more enchanting introduction to natural history for a child than to observe a family of hummingbirds in the nest. Maintain a distance, in order not to disturb them.

Butterflies

When I was a small child, my older sister told me that white butterflies were the souls of the dead. I believed her without doubt or hesitation, because she was eight years older, and infinitely wiser, than I. I was delighted to read, four decades later, this same bit of information in a book of Irish folklore. A century and a half since my family left the island, we still keep the lore going strong. At least, a little bit of it has survived.

The needs of butterflies are closely linked to the needs of the Folk. A garden well-designed for one will suit the needs of the other.

Ban all insecticides from your garden, if you wish to have either butterflies or the Folk in attendance. This includes such "organic," and therefore politically correct, substances as pyrethrin, neem, rotenone, and especially *Bacillus thuringensis*. Poison is as poison does. Killing caterpillars will not make butterflies welcome. If you want the gleam of gossamer wings in your yard, you will have to put up with holes in a few leaves. If your plantings are in danger of being defoliated, of course you may defend them. Instead of poisoning your garden, encourage hungry birds to take up residence by putting up birdhouses and feeders, and keeping the feeders stocked. Do not think that feeding the birds will make them less likely to eat the bugs that eat your flowers. Birds like a varied diet, and will relish the wrigglers that threaten your blooms. As in all things, balance is the key. A healthy backyard ecosystem is less likely to allow the devastation that often occurs when one species dominates the rest.

In order to optimize the butterfly population in your garden, provide plants that feed both the adults and the young. These will vary, according to the butterfly species that live in your area.

Good plants for caterpillars include beans, carrots, parsley, hollyhock and other mallows, and asclepias. Since you will be growing these specifically for the caterpillars, expect them to become quite bedraggled as they are eaten. Plant them well away from your decorative plants, since you do not want the caterpillars to become confused and eat your roses. Use floating row covers, which are filmy lengths of unwoven fabric available at garden centers or by mail, to protect any vegetable crops you want to harvest for your own use.

Adult butterflies tend to feed on flowers that are flat and open in shape. Among the best are butterfly bush (naturally), asters, daisies of the chrysanthemum family, asclepias, monardas, yarrow, feverfew, lantana, mint, verbena, and far too many weeds and wildflowers to list. If you have room enough, the butterflies—and the Folk—will appreciate a portion of the yard left unmowed, unweeded, untamed. For the sake of friendly relations with your human neighbors, it should be part of the yard that is hidden from the street.

chapter nine
sunshine

THE FOLK LOVE A NICE patch of well-tended lawn, and will patronize a yard that displays one, in preference to one that does not. Any low-growing ground cover can serve this purpose. While grass is most traditional in this country, and popular with the Folk, thyme can be even better. In France, many gardeners plant a bed of thyme specifically to attract the Folk, just as in this country we plant honeysuckle to bring hummingbirds. An area of flat, sunny lawn facilitates fairy dances and processions. That is to say, an area of *moonlit* lawn facilitates fairy dances and processions, since these invariably take place at night. If you wish to witness them, place your lawn area where it will be visible from inside the house, and be discreet. You do not wish the Folk to think you are spying on them.

chapter ten

shade

THERE SHOULD BE AT LEAST one tree in your fairy habitat, and at least one area in which the shrubs remain unpruned. This overgrown region provides shelter and privacy for the fauna of the garden. It is a place for the birds to nest, and for the Folk to rest in comfort.

While they are not mentioned in traditional lists of fairy plants, I find that the most popular plants in my yard include passion vine, mulberry, and Australian brush cherry. The latter two are such reliable nesting sites for birds, including hummingbirds, that I would not dream of disturbing them during the spring or summer. It is for the sake of the birds that I allowed the clipped hedge at the side of my house to go wild. Honest.

chapter eleven

water

A WATER FEATURE, HOWEVER SMALL, is essential in a fairy habitat. Whether bird or butterfly, lizard, frog, or pixie, every living thing needs water. If your garden offers it, then in your garden they will gather.

A water feature can be as simple as a clay saucer set on the ground, or as elaborate as a pond filled with koi and water lilies. All have their advantages. Natural, or natural-appearing, water features have the quality of welcoming wildlife on their own terms. Stones may be placed so that their hollows fill with water during rains, or when the garden is watered. Shallow ceramic saucers can be used in the same way. Shallow water features, preferably with dry rims, are especially useful to butterflies and small birds.

The familiar commercial birdbaths, on pedestals, make it more difficult for neighborhood cats to snack on your avian visitors. These should be placed in an area of open lawn, gravel, or other flat terrain, in order to eliminate the chance of cats pouncing from above.

Ponds can be formal or naturalistic. A great deal of trouble and expense is involved in creating a pond, so plan carefully before you begin. Do you want it to be visible from the house, so you can enjoy it from inside, or do you want it to be a surprise for visitors to come upon while wandering in the yard? This can be delightful, as long as it is designed to stumble *upon*, and not to stumble *into*. If you intend to grow water lilies, remember that they need full sun, and site your pond accordingly. If you want to raise koi, be aware that they need shade, which can be provided by the plants within the pond itself. Lest your koi become a buffet for local or migratory predators, you will need to devise a shelter for them. As an alternative, you can stock your pond with inexpensive "feeder" goldfish, and hope for predators. Great blue herons are rare where I live, and are only seen in the act of raiding ornamental fishponds.

chapter twelve

fragrance

THE FOLK ARE BEINGS who live by the pleasure of their senses, so be sure to provide pleasure for all the senses. It is easy to make a garden that is a continual scented delight, as many common garden plants smell good, and only a few, bad.

Many flowers are as valuable for their scents as for their visual beauty. Include with joy all the usual suspects. Roses, lilies, jasmine, narcissus, violets, and daphne all are wonderfully scented. If you wonder whether a particular variety is one of the best, buy it while it is in bloom. Your own nose would never lie to you.

Be sure to include plants with scented foliage. They will reliably scent your yard during the times, inevitable to even the best gardener, when there is nothing in bloom. Lavender, scented geraniums, bay trees, many citrus, and all culinary herbs qualify. Place these, unless they are thorny, close to paths, where you will brush against their leaves when you walk by. Stepping on a bit of mint that has escaped its bed to invade the lawn, or pulling weeds from around the lavender bed, makes even chores enjoyable.

The pleasure of a garden filled with flowers and herbs is beyond the power of words to express. Create one, and it will be filled with happy Folk.

Roses, especially, vary in the quality and potency of their fragrances. The usual rules of thumb are not always accurate. People who are not rose fanatics are frequently surprised to find that most red hybrid teas, to use the most obvious example, are completely scentless. Old, traditional varieties are not always more highly scented than modern ones, and roses that bloom only once per year are not always more fragrant than ones that bloom from Easter until first frost.

Even among roses that are famed for their remarkable scents, the pleasure they give you may vary. For instance, some of the roses bred by David Austin, internationally praised for their rare "myrrh" fragrance, smell to me like soap. Highest-quality, expensive soap, to be sure, but still, to my nose, more appropriate to the lavatory than the living room.

Something I have found out for myself is that purple roses always smell good. Do not take my word for it; go to a nursery or public rose garden, and smell for yourself.

chapter thirteen

artifacts

THE FOLK FIND HUMAN beings intriguing, as can be seen by their imitation of human rituals and human fashions. The Folk have been observed holding funerals, surely not necessary for an immortal race. They were enacting rituals they had witnessed among human beings, without comprehending their meaning. It is also common to see Folk dressed in contemporary fashion, or in the fashions of centuries past. Time means little to the Folk, and they sometimes become confused as to the time frame in which we live.

While you are working to preserve the illusion of wilderness in part of your garden, be sure to give evidence of a human presence in others. Articles of human manufacture will not discourage the Folk from visiting your garden, and may serve as intriguing invitations to them.

An acquaintance of mine, who summers in an old log cabin in the forest, places tiny model houses in the crotches of nearby trees, and populates them with ceramic gnomes. She reports good success in luring the Folk. A neighbor hides toys and model animals, from the garden center, along a path around her flower beds. She tells me that they are there for her grandchildren to find, but her garden is certainly the most magical place in our neighborhood. Serious statuary and formal urns have their place, as do items that can only be described as silly. I consider myself a person of sophistication and taste, but there are two pair of plastic flamingos in my garage, waiting to be placed on my lawn. They will become part of a tableau for the winter holidays, I think.

Celebration of seasonal change will also serve to intrigue the Folk. Another neighbor decorates her yard, not only for the winter holidays and for Halloween, as might be expected, but for all the holidays and seasonal changes throughout the year. All this effort on her part makes the Folk feel warmly welcomed, as it does the rest of the neighborhood.

Everything placed in the garden as a lure to the Folk does not have to be new, nor does it have to be old. Eccentricity is a positive boon. My mother, who was born and raised on a tropical island, lined her borders with seashells. When my father took up rock collecting as a hobby, she added chunks of amethyst, jade, and petrified wood. Here is another general concept: By decorating your yard to celebrate your personal interests, history, and ethnic background, you welcome the individual sprites who will be most sympathetic to you.

chapter fourteen

time

THE FOLK ARE ENAMORED of time. Time flows differently in Faerie as is shown by the raft of stories about people who have spent a brief time with the Folk, and returned to find that hundreds of years have passed. The Folk are fascinated by human beings and our circumstances. Since their world is seasonless and eternal, a garden that emphasizes seasonal ebb and flow is irresistible to them. The following lists of plants are by no means exhaustive, but are only meant as starting points for your own imagination.

To emphasize spring, plant daffodils, viburnum, calla lilies, deciduous fruit trees, hardenbergia, once-blooming roses, and ranunculuses.

To emphasize summer, plant crape myrtles, oriental lilies, sunflowers, butterfly bush (buddleia), naked ladies (lycoris), and senna.

To emphasize fall, plant Japanese anemones, chrysanthemums, maples, liquidambers, mulberries, and princess flowers.

To emphasize winter, plant hollies, pyracanthas, camellias, conifers of all kinds, deciduous trees with architectural forms, hellebores, and witchhazel.

part three

magical combinations:

sample garden designs

chapter fifteen

utopia

THIS IS AN EVOCATION of coastal Northern California. Redwood forests are among the most magical places on Earth, the homes of myriad happy Folk. I have felt the acute presence of the Folk even in second-growth redwood forests, where the stumps of logged-out trees have resprouted and grown up into rings of adolescents a hundred feet tall. The eerie silence and cool of a redwood forest can be re-created even in a suburban setting, if you have enough room, enough water, and a willingness to devote your whole yard to shade. The spell cast by a single redwood tree is as extensive as its shadow.

While redwoods are native to cool, damp coastal regions, they grow well even in hot, dry climates, if given sufficient irrigation when they are young. If you have an enormous yard, plant the trees ten feet apart in a circle. If your yard is only large, one or two redwood trees in the southern corners of the yard will give plenty of shade and enchantment. This is not a look for a small yard. Even a single redwood will outgrow a small yard within several years, casting a feeling of doom, instead of the desired enchantment.

To add color and liveliness to the glade, plant shade-tolerant varieties of iris and orchid, along with ferns. Little more than that grows in a real redwood grove, nor is any more needed. Less authentic, but also beautiful, are fuschias, impatiens, begonias, and hostas or aspidistras.

The best water feature for a redwood garden is a running stream or waterfall. If that cannot be arranged, a small fountain of rustic design will do. The most appropriate sensible artifact would be a hand-hewn wooden bench. One of those bears carved out of a single log with a chainsaw is regionally appropriate, if you can bear (no pun intended) the sheer silliness of it.

spanish mission

THE GARDEN DESCRIBED HERE evokes the Southwest of the United States during the period from the eighteenth century until the early part of the twentieth. It is a style that has regained its popularity recently, for a variety of reasons. It requires less use of supplemental irrigation than other traditional styles of garden, without compromising on issues of beauty. It requires little care, and no use of toxic chemicals, as the plants listed are all tough and resistant to disease and pests. While the plants listed are subtropicals, able to tolerate only a few degrees of freezing, they are not difficult to use in a colder climate. Dwarf citrus trees can be grown in tubs without difficulty, and brought into a frost-free location, such as a sunny window or enclosed porch, for the winter. Hardy varieties of roses can be substituted for the tender varieties that are most historically appropriate for a Southwestern garden. Herbs, such as rosemary and Mexican sage, grow quickly enough to be replaced annually in climates where they do not winter over.

This is a garden concept that can be used to good effect in a yard of any size, even in a patio or enclosed courtyard. Indeed, the palaces of the Moorish rulers of Spain always included an enclosed court-yard with a fountain. These courtyards were considered to be evocative of Paradise. As such, they are certainly appropriate sur-roundings for the sort of Folk with whom we strive to share our homes and lives.

The only requirement for Mediterranean gardens such as these is sunlight. If your climate tends to be overcast, this garden plan will be most successful if you site it where it will get a full day of sun. In a very sunny climate, such as that of Spain, Italy, or Los Angeles, a half day of sun will be sufficient, though less than ideal.

Citrus trees are the envy of the northern world, and an original source of wealth in the warm regions to which they are best suited. Before railroads, they were rare and expensive treats, limited to the holidays for all but the wealthiest families. It was not so long ago that my family always put a tangerine in the toe of each Christmas stock-ing. This was the invariant tradition, even though we had lived in a citrus-growing region for two generations already.

All citrus trees are beautiful, if well cared for. They hold their shiny, deep green leaves throughout the year, and are remarkably fragrant when in bloom. I am told that some of the more ethereal of the Folk live on fragrance as their only sustenance, so it is good to provide an abundance of pleasant aromas. If you are in a region warm enough that they can be grown outdoors, any standard or semidwarf citrus tree can be the centerpiece of your garden. If you are doubtful of your climate, however, and want to plant citrus trees in the ground, ask at the nursery before you buy, because different species and varieties vary in their tolerance to frost.

For growing in tubs, I especially recommend Nagami kumquat and Meyer lemons, grown on dwarfing rootstock.

The Nagami kumquat grows only three or four feet tall, and holds its brightly colored orange fruits for much of the year. The fruit may be eaten whole, including the peel. The peel is sweet and aromatic, while the flesh is as tart as lemons. Biting into one is something of a shock. They are also good for making marmalade, if you have the inclination to do so. In China, kumquats grown in pots were used as table decorations for feasts and given as gifts to honored guests. They make ideal focal points for miniature landscapes, with scale-model buildings and inhabitants around them. Conceits such as these are well suited to gaining the interest of the Folk.

The Meyer lemon is also commonly grown as a dwarf in pots. The fruit is very choice, golden in color, and slightly sweeter and more fragrant than common supermarket lemons. In recent years, they have become fashionable, commanding astronomical prices on the menus of trendy restaurants, and in chic farmers' markets. This recent development amuses me, as Meyer lemons have been around for decades as the quintessential backyard lemon of the Southwest. Every glass of lemonade of my childhood was made with Meyer lemons. Now, Meyer lemonade goes for several dollars per bottle, in only the best places. Some individual Meyer lemon trees are reported to bear fruit year-round, but I find that they bear only during the winter and spring. Their flower buds, in the spring, look like slightly elongated pearls streaked with lavender. I have seen, on occasion, little lavender and white spiders living among their leaves, only at this time of year. They resemble the buds exactly, and are never seen when the buds are absent.

On the fences, grow climbing roses. If your climate is mild enough, dropping no more than a few degrees below the freezing point, grow the roses historically favored in the Mediterranean and in those parts of the United States that boast a Mediterranean climate. The most appropriate would be Belle Portugaise, Climbing Cecile Brunner, or any of the Lady Banks roses. Unfortunately, Belle Portugaise and the Lady Banks varieties are strictly once-blooming, and the Climbing Cecile Brunner does not repeat reliably. These are all space hogs as well, suitable only where you have plenty of room. In a smaller garden, use the original, nonclimbing variety of Cecile Brunner, which does repeat reliably for most of the year.

Belle Portugaise sports large, semidouble blooms of the palest pink, which droop silkily from the branches overhead. Because the flowers droop (they are supposed to), it should always be planted where it will be seen from below.

Climbing Cecile Brunner bears perfect buttonhole roses only an inch long. They start out in perfect tea rose form, opening the next day into tiny pompoms. The plant is vigorous to a fault, covering a space fifteen feet across in a year or two. With training, it will happily grow thirty feet into a tree. It is harder to get it to behave itself, in the sense of staying politely in one place. Plant it only where you have room. It is excellent at covering ugly old woodsheds, and at keeping neighborhood children from climbing fences where it grows. As it is as thorny as most roses, it provides good supplemental security. For six weeks or so in the spring, it covers itself with its blossoms, thousands of them, creating a scene of great enchantment. Later in the summer, it may bring forth a stray blossom or two, but a shrub the size of a mature Climbing Cecile Brunner needs more than one or two one-inch blooms to be properly ornamented.

The original variety Cecile Brunner, which forms a neat shrub only three feet high and wide, has blooms identical to its mutant offspring. It carries them throughout the growing season, and does not aspire to world domination. I like the climber, partly for sentimental reasons. It was discovered, over a hundred years ago, in a town where I used to live. I am willing to admit, however, that the original is much better where space is limited.

There are four Lady Banks roses: single white, single yellow, double white, and double yellow. They are reputed to smell like violets, but some sources say that only the yellow ones are scented, some that only the white ones are scented, and some that only the singles have a discernable fragrance. I have grown both the yellow doubles and the white doubles, and am unable to detect any perfume in either. They bloom very early in the spring, sometimes as early as the end of January. They bloom continuously for two or three months, after which there is no further bloom until the next year. They are just as vigorous as the Climbing Cecile Brunner, but are entirely thornless. They are good at covering chain-link fences and hiding the neighbor's garage from view. Their best quality is blooming before anything else in the garden, bringing color and beauty to the ragged end of winter and the muddy days of spring.

One word of caution, should you choose to grow the white, double form of the Lady Banks rose. It is very hard to find. What is usually labeled as such is actually Fortuniana. If you are insistent on planting the real white Lady Banks, buy it in person, while it is in bloom. The flowers should be ruffled, half an inch across, in clusters exactly like those of the yellow Lady Banks. If, instead, you see cup-shaped blooms that are one and a half inches across, and arranged singly along the stem, you have a Fortuniana.

If your garden is too cold to accommodate the abovementioned roses, choose one that is casual in form, for this kind of garden. Hybrid perpetuals and hybrid teas are too formal for the somewhat eccentric look we are going for here. Any of the rugosas would look good, as would the hardy roses bred specifically for the North such as the Griffith Buck roses or the Explorer series from Canada.

Roses have been included in the gardens of every people that has sought to attract the Folk. Even in India, where roses sulk in the heat and succumb to disease, goddesses and sprites are believed to be made of roses. With a nod to practicality, these rose-petal goddesses are honored with gifts of water lilies, which are much easier to grow in the tropics.

Giant aloes or other giant succulents, as climate and availability dictate, sing welcome to the Folk, especially in combination with roses and citrus trees, as mentioned above. They are frost-tender and usually hard to find for sale, so substitution may be necessary.

Smaller aloes are readily available, grow equally well in pots or in the ground, and are just as attractive to hummingbirds and other native Folk. They are just less stylish than their giant brethren. An aloe in bloom, outside the kitchen window, can even make washing dishes pleasant.

For herbal scents and a long season of bloom (which are good for drawing birds, butterflies, and the Folk), plant rosemary and any of the shrubby varieties of sage. There are myriad varieties of each. Rosemary can grow upright to four feet high, or flat against the ground. The flowers can be any shade of blue, white, or pink. The leaves are a good seasoning in cooking, and the stems of the upright varieties make flavorsome skewers for use in barbecuing. Sages come in shades of purple, blue, and red. I find the purples and reds to be easier to grow and less demanding than the blues, but I continue to grow the blues for the purity and intensity of their color. Mexican sage, which has amusing purple flowers that look as if they were fashioned from velour, is indispensable for its ease of care, reliability, length of bloom, attractiveness to hummingbirds, and fragrant foliage. I also like to include at least one of the red perennial sages, such as pineapple sage. The hummingbirds love it.

To complete the picture, include such wild annuals as California poppies and red flax. These are easily grown from seed. Just prepare the ground by loosening up the top several inches of soil with a shovel or garden fork, and scatter the seeds lightly on the surface. Water gently every day until the seedlings appear, and you have your annual wildflowers well underway. Once the plants are three or four inches tall, you will need to water them only when the soil becomes very dry. They are likely to reseed themselves, making the garden self-perpetuating.

Where winters are mild, plant your annual wildflowers in the fall, after the weather cools off, to take advantage of winter rains and cooler growing temperatures. If you plant in the fall, you will not have to water as often. The seeds will decide for themselves when to germinate and when to bloom, based on temperatures, day lengths, and rain. Where winters are cold, sow the seeds in earliest spring, as soon as the snow has melted. If the seedlings are cut down by late frosts, plant again when the weather has settled. Seed is cheap, and planting it is easy, so you do not lose much by gambling on an early spring.

Mulch the beds with crushed stone. The best possible water feature would be a reflecting pond or fountain lined with colorful tiles, such as are found in Mexico, Spain, and Italy. As these can be prohibitively expensive, you may certainly opt for a pedestal birdbath or small fountain. Colorful ones imported from Mexico can be obtained for a reasonable sum. A spa or swimming pool is the usual accompaniment to this style of garden in California, but is of limited use to the Folk.

Budget permitting, a substantial built-in barbecue is both traditional and appropriate for this style of garden. Nothing contributes to the misery of a hot summer like cooking indoors, which is why families that could not flee to the mountains, the beach, or a northern state always kept "summer kitchens" in their backyards in the days before air conditioning. While the Folk of northern lands may not recognize the barbecue from the Old Country, Folk from sunnier climes will appreciate the implication of hospitality. Let it be more than an implication: entertain frequently outdoors, as the friendly Folk universally love a party, and the malevolent sorts cannot abide them.

chapter seventeen

prairie

THE PRAIRIE GARDEN EVOKES the central region of North America. It is open, mostly sunny, and very easy to maintain. It is suitable for any climate, without the drudge work of bringing poorly adapted plants indoors for the winter.

For shade, plant a poplar that is well adapted to your soil and climate. Most poplars will live in all but the most extreme climates, but two of the most beautiful, which also have the most emotive value, are more particular. The Fremont cottonwood, beloved sign-post of Western oases and desert homesteads, loves heat but will not tolerate cold. The quaking aspen, loveliest of mountain trees and golden beacon of autumn, loves cold winters but languishes and dies where summers are hot and winters mild.

The heart of a Prairie garden is in its open spaces. Instead of a conventional lawn, choose dwarf grasses native to your area, or well adapted to it, and leave them unmown. Since you will not be mowing your "lawn," it will be simple to scatter wildfower seed directly among the grasses. Rudbeckia and echinacea are good choices, if not indispensable. To this base, add whatever flowers are closest to your heart or locale. Bluebonnets, poppies, owl's clover all add to the color and charm of the scene. You already know the pull that wildflowers exert on all sensitive creatures.

This is the garden in which to plant an old-fashioned, shrubby sort of rose, such as a Ragged Robin or a Harrison's Yellow. Ragged Robin blooms heavily throughout the growing season, with light red, semidouble flowers. Harrison's Yellow blooms only once, in the early summer, but is loved for its historical associations. It is widely identified as the "Yellow Rose of Texas," although the song clearly refers to a woman.

The water feature of the Prairie garden should be something rustic, something associated with farming or ranching. A trough, such as is used for watering horses, would be ideal, as would a copper wash boiler or a half barrel. Let your pocketbook, and local availability, be your guides. Appropriate artifacts would be agricultural antiques, which are, unfortunately, astronomically expensive. Aged, rusty, and possibly broken gardening tools, however, can be picked up for a song at any yard sale or flea market, and are better suited to performing as ornaments than as implements.

chapter eighteen

woodland

THIS GARDEN LEANS TOWARD the shade, as the Prairie garden leans toward the sun. It is a place of cool retreat, more suitable for smaller gardens than the redwood-based Utopian plan.

For an evergreen background to the scene, I favor a Japanese pine. I love the sight of blue sky seen through long pine needles. Any conifer suited to your climate will work as well.

In front of the conifers, granting summer shade while allowing winter sun, plant Japanese maples. No, I am not going for an Asian theme here, just a smaller tree than the maples typically grown as shade trees on extensive estates. They come in myriad colors and forms.

Any dogwood suitable to your climate would be a good understory tree. They enjoy either shade or sun in most of their range. All are good wildlife trees. Some bear edible fruit, which is always an advantage.

Grass will not grow in deep shade, so plan to pave the areas on which you will be walking. Natural materials, such as brick, stone, gravel, or even a thick layer of bark mulch, work best. For color, plant hellebores, Johnny-jump-ups, violets, daffodils, and impatiens. Most of the flowers will perform best in areas where they will receive winter sun. Plant them under the maples, not under the pines. Ferns and hostas or aspidistras will increase the air of serenity.

A naturalistic pond would be the best water feature for a woodland garden, space allowing. A birdbath set low to the ground would also fit in well, as would hollow stones, sited to catch the rain.

I always like to include evidence of human habitation when designing a habitat for the Folk, in order to attract the Folk who are friendly to human beings, and to discourage those who are not. In this garden the most suitable artifact would be a few comfortable chairs and a table for a beverage or two. This garden is too pretty to go unused.

chapter nineteen

farmyard

THE FAIR FOLK ARE ADMIRERS of human industry and the agrarian lifestyle. Simulating a working farmyard will delight them, and give you plenty of flowers and veggies for the house.

Use deciduous fruit trees liberally for this garden. According to your tastes and climate, choose from among apples, cherries, peaches, plums, apricots, almonds. They are all members of the rose family, all widely adapted, all beautiful in bloom, all generous with their bounty. Many varieties are widely available on dwarfing rootstocks, so many individual trees can fit even in a fairly small yard. In climates where the chosen trees are marginal, they can in many cases still be used as ornamentals. For instance, it is much too warm in my climate to grow cherries for their fruit. I continue to grow them for their graceful forms and clouds of spring blossoms. They never disappoint in that regard, although I know that I can expect fruit from them only in very cold years.

Shrubby, old-fashioned roses are entirely appropriate in this design. Many working farms and orchards are surrounded by split-rail fences draped in colorful roses chosen by farmer or spouse.

These are sometimes rationalized as attractants for bees, needed to pollinate the crop plants. This does not make perfect sense. Citrus orchards, the most common large-scale farms in my home range, cover acre after acre. Their fragrant, open blossoms must certainly be more attractive to pollinating insects than a narrow line of roses, especially if they are the fully double types of roses that do not even offer nectar. I think they are more attractive to the people who plant them for their color and scent. They are equally attractive to the Folk, who love them for the same reasons we do.

In any case, plant healthy varieties of roses that do not require spraying. You will have a lot of edibles in this garden, which you will not want to contaminate with fungicides. The roses themselves can be among the edibles. While the aromatic flavor takes some getting used to, the petals make elegant sandwiches with good bread and a little butter. They can also be used to make an unusual jam, which you can purchase at Greek markets to sample. Rosewater is a common dessert and beverage flavoring in the Middle East. Rose hips are an excellent source of vitamin C, and a tangy addition to pies, jams, and teas.

The rose family extends further, to blackberries and raspberries to train on fences, and strawberries to cover the ground with a charming succession of foliage, flowers, and fruit. Just one fence planted with boysenberries is enough to garner you many invitations to Fourth of July potluck suppers. Plunge deeply into the rose family, and reap the results.

More edible ornamentals include sunflowers, tomatoes, chiles, eggplants, chard, beets, asparagus, herbs, and whatever else your heart or taste buds desire. Do not worry whether they will look good. All healthy plants look good, and a well-tended vegetable garden is a beautiful thing.

A lawn is not appropriate in this garden, which is a boon for those who are allergic to grass, or just do not want to care for it. Trodden earth is a perfectly good surface for paths, if your soil does not tend toward mud. If it does, a dressing of sand or gravel will solve the problem.

A scarecrow or windmill will provide ornamentation enough. Bales of straw can provide seating until they begin to break down, at which time they can be used as mulch or added to the compost pile. A fountain in the shape of a pump would look as lovely as it is appropriate, sited over a half barrel or trough.

The Folk love a kitchen garden, and will increase its yield as they increase its liveliness.

cottage garden

THE ESSENCE OF A COTTAGE GARDEN is to pack the most possible garden into the available space. There will be flowers and fruit, vegetables and ornaments, all packed together as tightly as the needs of the plants will allow. The keyword here is not restraint, but exuberance.

The cottage garden is the type most fitting for the Folk of the British Isles, the pre-Celtic Folk most familiar to American students of folklore. This is the sort of garden most likely to draw the elves, brownies, leprechauns, and others with whom we are so long-familiar that we just call them generically "fairies," as we would call our own human tribe simply "people."

This garden requires ample water, a modicum of labor, and a climate with mild summers. The flowers that are most well-loved in the British Isles neither need nor tolerate extreme heat. In return, it will give you food, flowers, and enchantment.

For shade, any of the trees listed previously as magical will serve. In addition, elm, birch, and sycamore are traditional options. There will be no room for a proper lawn, but grassy paths are expected.

Roses are an absolute requirement, as are lilies. For the roses, the shrubby, fully double, and heavily scented varieties are the ones wanted. Any of the hybrid perpetuals would be suitable, as would any of the Bourbon roses. Climate allowing, this would be an appropriate place for Gallicas, Centifolias, or the more elaborate Albas, if you are willing to sacrifice repeat bloom. Best of all would be the modern hybrids designed to look like the classics, but with a wider color range and repeat bloom. These are represented by the Austin's English roses, the French Romanticas, and others. The lilies should be similarly old-fashioned, without necessarily being old varieties.

Among the roses and lilies should be, according to your climate and tastes, daisies, peonies, iris, hollyhocks, geraniums, achillea, rosemary, lavender, sage, thyme, and clematis. Foxgloves and delphiniums are well known for their association with the Folk. Lewis Carroll, in *The Nursery Alice*, explains, "The right word is 'Folk's-Gloves.' Did you ever hear that Fairies used to be called 'the good Folk'?" Many folklorists agree with this association. In addition, foxglove is a traditional remedy for "dropsy," now known as congestive heart failure. Digitalis, a drug originally derived from foxglove, is one of the most effective treatments for congestive heart failure to this day. As previously noted, healing is magical, and magic implies the involvement of the Folk.

Among these, plant tomatoes, lettuces, beets, chard, carrots, spinach, and whatever else you like. As with the farmyard garden, it is important not to use toxins of any kind near edibles.

final word on inspiration

SPEND TIME OUTDOORS TO GET inspiration for your garden. Seek out magical locations close to your home, and look for clues to establishing an attractive environment for the Folk native to your area.

If you live on the edge of a wilderness, it will be easy to find such a place. The air will seem particularly crystalline; your thoughts will clear. Your mind will drift to thoughts of love and happiness. When this happens, look around. What do you see? Is there a flat rock where you can lie on your back and look at the blue sky through a tracery of sycamore leaves? Is there the sound of running water? Are there small plants growing in the crevices of a rock wall? All of these effects can be evoked in the garden, if not precisely duplicated. A raised area of deck can stand in for the flat rock. A fountain can provide the sound of running water. Any one of a number of trees can provide an open canopy through which to view the sky.

If you live in an established city or suburb, you can still find suitable fairy habitats close to home. The Folk are as adaptable in their requirements as we are. People can live from Nome to Casablanca, and so can the Folk. In the older parts of town, look for the gardens that have history. Look for signs of enchantment, just as you would in the woods. Does one alley draw you back repeatedly, or a friend's terrace, or the patio of a favorite restaurant? It does not take much room to create a setting that will attract the Folk. A small garden, or a small portion of a larger one, allows greater intimacy.

Now you know enough to begin to create a welcoming home for the Folk in your own home. Doing so will increase the comfort and joy and peace in your life. Begin now.

blessed be.

glossary

Brownies Friendly Folk who help with the household chores.

Cultivar Short for "cultivated variety." Each specimen of a cultivar is genetically identical to every other.

Dripline The imaginary circle directly beneath a tree's outermost branches.

Faerie The realm of the Folk. It overlaps and interpenetrates our own.

Folk of the Host Folk who go about their business at night, indifferent to the human beings around them.

Friend In a gardening context, a related variety of plant that serves as a pollen source.

Glamour The ability of the Folk to make things appear as something other than what they are. There are many old stories of the Folk disguising old women as young, mushrooms as beef, and dried leaves as gold.

Karma The accumulated actions, for good or ill, that cling to one's soul.

Roan The people of the sea. They can take the shape of seals while in the water, and human beings while on land. They sometimes intermarry with human beings.

Selkies Like the Roan, Selkies are magical beings from the sea who can assume the form of either a seal or a human being.

Understory The community of plants that live in the shade of tall trees.

recommended reading

THE FOLLOWING ARE THE BOOKS I have found most useful in preparing this one. I have acquired my library over many years, so some of them are out of print. I list them anyway, as they are sometimes reissued. They can also be found in used bookstores, in well-stocked libraries, and over the Internet.

I list them in descending order of usefulness for a person new to the topic. In other words, read the first book listed first. Go on to the others as long as your curiosity remains unsatisfied.

folklore

Froud, Brian and Lee, Alan. *Faeries*. Harry N. Abrams, 1978. This is still in print. It is easy to read, delightful to look at, and absolutely accurate. It is the best possible entry into the study of the Folk.

Briggs, Katharine. *An Encyclopedia of Fairies*. Random House, 1976. An exhaustive listing, alphabetically arranged, of European folklore. Its sole flaw is that it is hard to stop reading, which may lead to missed appointments and insomnia.

Keightley, Thomas. *The Fairy Mythology*. G. Bell, 1880. It was reissued as

The World Guide to Gnomes, Fairies, Elves, and Other Little People, Avenel Books, 1978. Did I describe the work above as exhaustive? This is even more so. It is a serious work of scholarship.

Evans-Wentz, W. Y. *The Fairy Faith in Celtic Countries*. Oxford University Press, 1911. Reissued by Colin Smythe Limited in 1977. Dedicated to A.E. and William Butler Yeats, this is a true gem of the Celtic Renaissance. Were it a river, it would be an impossibility: it is both dry and deep. If you manage to read it all the way through, you will have learned something.

Yeats, William Butler. *Irish Folk Tales*. The edition I used was printed in 1973 by The Cardavon Press, but no worries. It is frequently reprinted, and should be available at any large bookstore.

General gardening

Sunset Western Garden Book, by a great phalanx of the editors of the first and best lifestyle magazine of the western u.s., *Sunset*. If, under pain of death, I were forced to give up all my books but one, this is the one I would keep. East of the Rockies, it is just one more garden book: a useful encyclopedia of plants, but without the biblical status it carries in the West. There is now a Northeastern version titled, naturally, *Sunset Northeastern Garden Book*.

Ellis, Barbara W., Benjamin, Joan, and Martin, Deborah. *Rodale's Low-Maintenance Gardening Techniques*. Rodale Press, 1995. A useful book, containing only habitat-friendly techniques. Not region-specific.

Benjamin, Joan and Martin, Deborah. *Great Garden Formulas*. Rodale Press, 1998. This book contains recipes for every possible nontoxic means of pest control, as well as recipes for homegrown herbal cosmetics, and the address of every mail-order nursery in the known world. Worth having.

Murray, Elizabeth. *Cultivating Sacred Space*. Pomegranate, 1997. What a beautiful book! Sensitively explores the relationship between spirituality and garden design.

Habitat gardening

Dennis, John V. and McKinley, Michael. *How to Attract Birds*. Ortho Books, 1995. This is one of the meatier books in the genre.

Lewis, Alcinda, ed. *Butterfly Gardens*. Brooklyn Botanic Garden, 1997. Not much more than a listing of butterflies and the plants that attract them. Even so, it is the best book of its kind available.

Schneck, Marcus. *Creating a Hummingbird Garden*. Simon & Schuster, 1993. Surprisingly full of information for such a small book.

———. *Creating a Butterfly Garden*. Simon & Schuster, 1993. What I just said.